FREE NELSON
MANDELA

FREE NELSON MANDELA

FESTIVAL CONCERT BOOK

TEXT BY MARY BENSON AND LIZ NICKSON
FOREWORD BY WINNIE MANDELA

PENGUIN BOOKS

PENGUIN BOOKS

Published by the Penguin Group
27 Wrights Lane, London W8 5TZ, England
Viking Penguin Inc., 40 West 23rd Street, New York, New York 10010, USA
Penguin Books Australia Ltd, Ringwood, Victoria, Australia
Penguin Books Canada Ltd, 2801 John Street, Markham, Ontario, Canada L3R 1BA
Penguin Books (NZ) Ltd, 182-190 Wairau Road, Auckland 10, New Zealand

Penguin Books Ltd, Registered Offices: Harmondsworth, Middlesex, England

First published 1988
10 9 8 7 6 5 4 3 2 1

Produced by Michael Rainbird Publishing Limited 55–56 St Martin's Lane,
London WC2N 4EA

Designed by Laurence Bradbury and Roy Williams
With help from Roger Pring, Dorothy Tucker, Paul Levy, Gurdip Bhandal,
Hannah Moore, Kevin Smith, Penny Philips, Craig Cornock, David Mallott,
Rob Partridge, Brian Rooney, Colin Woodman

Captions by Rob Partridge

Photographic co-ordination by Chalkie Davies

Portrait photography by Davies and Starr

Panoramic photography by Laurie Lewis

Live and backstage photography by
Adrian Boot, Mike Putland, Paul Rider, Stefan Wallgren, Dave Wainwright,
Justin Thomas, Laurie Lewis, Dario Mitidieri, Duncan Raban, Kevin Cummins,
Alan Davidson, Dave Hogan, Eugene Adabari, Paul Roberts, Tim Jarvis

Typesetting by Jigsaw Graphics
Filmset in Walbaum 8½/15

Origination by John Dixon & Co Ltd

Made and printed in Great Britain by
Cooper Clegg Web Offset Ltd
Ashchurch, Gloucestershire

Cover design by Laurence Bradbury and Roy Williams

Back cover, title page painting: John N. Muafangejo
Half title painting: Keith Haring

CONTENTS

A MESSAGE TO NELSON MANDELA

FROM ARCHBISHOP TREVOR HUDDLESTON C.R.
PRESIDENT OF THE ANTI-APARTHEID MOVEMENT

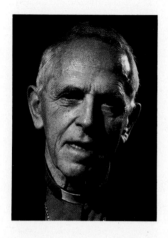

The message from Wembley rang loud and clear – Free Nelson Mandela. It came from the artists on stage. It came from the crowd of 72,000 packed into the Stadium as they roared back the chant. And it was echoed in hundreds of millions of homes across the world as they watched or listened to the broadcast. The memory of Jerry Dammers performing 'Free Nelson Mandela' with the crowd chanting back 'the whole world is watching' is unforgettable. Today the whole world is watching P.W. Botha. Will he unlock the prison doors? Will he free Nelson Mandela? Will he free the children? Will he release all the political prisoners and detainees?

My dear Nelson, the world will no longer tolerate your continued imprisonment. You can and must be freed. The artists of the world rallied together at Wembley to pay tribute to you. For this I am immensely grateful. Today the people of the world are united as never before in seeking your freedom and that of your people. But now is the time for the peoples and governments of the world to act. Our great 'Nelson Mandela: Freedom at 70' campaign, of which the Wembley Tribute was just the first highlight, is galvinizing people into action the length and breadth of Britain and throughout the world. I am confident that we will succeed.

My thoughts and prayers are always with you and your dear wife Winnie.

＋ Trevor Huddleston CR

TREVOR HUDDLESTON C.R.

FOREWORD

BY NOMZAMO WINNIE MANDELA

June 11, 1988 is a date which will be written indelibly into the history of our freedom struggle. The great gathering in Wembley Stadium of artists from all over the world to pay tribute to our cause was a source of great inspiration to all our people. The knowledge that their message reached into the homes of millions of people across the globe gave it even greater significance. We are grateful to all the artists who performed at Wembley and for all those who made the event possible. It has given us renewed hope and confidence that the doors of the prisons of apartheid can be forced open and Mandela and his colleagues set free. We now know with complete certainty that the whole world is with us in our struggle. That was the real message to all of us from Wembley.

Our spirits were with you in Wembley even though we could not be with you in person. And I know that our leaders in prison felt the same. I was very moved when Father Huddleston and Oliver Tambo phoned me directly from the Stadium. They were able to convey to me something of the atmosphere and the spirit of the people. I could hear in the background the trombone of our own Jonas Gwangwa as he played the music from 'Cry Freedom'.

We are delighted to be able to write this foreword. This pictorial and written record of the Wembley Concert provides a further opportunity for our message to reach across the world. It is our cherished hope that all these efforts will secure the freedom of all our leaders and that of our people. Let us join hands in ridding the world of the scourge of apartheid and racism. Let freedom triumph.

Winnie Mandela

N.W. MANDELA

INTRODUCTION

The Rock Concert celebrated the seventieth birthday of the world's most famous political prisoner, Nelson Mandela. Since his imprisonment in August 1962, he has embodied the struggle for freedom in South Africa. Despite the South African government's efforts to eradicate his influence – in that country it is illegal to quote him or to display his portrait – most South Africans, among them young people born long after he had vanished into jail, regard him as their authentic leader. Mandela would be the first to insist that he should not be singled out from all those who have fought

for justice – men, women and children – many of whom have sacrificed their lives. But, as the Commonwealth Group of Eminent Persons said after visiting South Africa in 1986, he has become a 'living legend'...a potent inspiration for much of the political activity of Black South Africans . . . His suffering is seen as the suffering of all who are the victims of apartheid. The campaign for his release has been the galvanizing spur for rising Black political consciousness across South Africa...the centrepiece of the demand for a political settlement.'

Internationally, Mandela has been widely honoured. Together with the King of

Nelson Mandela with Mary Benson, London 1962.

Youths demanding the release of political prisoners.

His suffering is ... the suffering of all who are the victims of apartheid

At the unveiling of the Mandela bust at the Festival Hall: Zenani Mandela Dlamini and Oliver Tambo.

Mandela's hut at the Royal Place, Tembuland.

Spain he was awarded Venezuela's Simón Bolívar Prize, and other prizes have come from Spain, Austria, Cuba and Sweden. Cities in Scotland and Italy, in Greece, Belgium and Australia, have conferred 'freedom' on him. Streets, parks, buildings and squares have been named after him. Universities in New York, Lesotho, Brussels, Lancaster, Zimbabwe, Michigan and Havana have conferred honorary degrees, while students' unions have elected him an honorary member. Poems and songs extol his life and, like many heads of government and 2,000 mayors in fifty-three countries, call for his release.

Born into the royal family of the Tembu people in the Transkei, Mandela was named Rolihlahla, a Xhosa word which has been interpreted as 'stirring up trouble'. During a traditional childhood, even as he herded cattle and helped with the plough-ing, he longed for adventure and was capti-vated by tales of heroic ancestors who had defended their land against European invaders. His first encounter with Euro-pean education was disconcerting. At the Methodist school, the white woman teacher asked his name and he told her, 'Rolihlahla.' 'What!' He repeated it, whereupon she declared, 'You will be called Nelson.' (Friends and comrades, however, address him by his clan name, Madiba.) He went on to study at the prestigious college for Blacks, Fort Hare, only to be suspended after three years for taking part in a students' strike. Then, in 1941, he turned his back on an arranged marriage and the prospect of chieftainship, and ran away from the comparative tranquility of the rural Transkei 'Reserve' to Johannesburg – Egoli, city of gold.

A tall, striking, athletic, still unsophisti-cated, rather aloof young man, he soon learned the bitter facts of life for Africans under the colour bar imposed by the White minority government. 'Natives' were denied all human rights and were confined to 'locations' and shanty towns where most lived in poverty. Overcrowded, insanitary, without electricity, tarred roads or tele-phones, these urban slums were conti-nually raided by police. Mandela's political

Mandela was named Rolihlahla ... meaning 'stirring up trouble'

education had begun.

Encouraged by a new friend, Walter Sisulu, he studied law and, after qualifying as an attorney (solicitor), formed a partnership with Oliver Tambo, who had been a fellow-student at Fort Hare. To their office came a stream of victims of the apartheid system. The two young lawyers and Sisulu had already taken the first step towards dedicating their lives to their people by joining the African National Congress. Founded in 1912, the ANC had continually protested against one injustice after another, protests ignored by successive governments. Now Sisulu, Mandela and Tambo became a remarkable political team as they created a Youth League with other African nationalists. They were determined to galvanize the somewhat conservative ANC into militant, but non-violent, action against the powerful Afrikaner Nationalist Government.

In 1952 Mandela was appointed Volunteer-in-Chief of the Defiance campaign when 8,500 men and women – most of them African but with significant support from Indians and a handful of Whites – deliberately broke apartheid laws and went to jail. He and Sisulu were among the leaders convicted under the Suppression of Communism Act. In giving them nine-month suspended sentences, the Judge agreed that the charge had nothing to do with communism 'as it is commonly known', and accepted evidence that they had consistently advised their followers 'to avoid violence in any shape or form'. But the government was set on an ever more repressive course. Mandela, described by Oliver Tambo as a born mass leader, was elected President of the Transvaal ANC, only to be banned from all political activity

The ANC had continually protested against one injustice after another

The young lawyers, Tambo and Mandela.

African demands at the Congress of the People, 1955.

Mandela and his bride, Winnie Nomzamo Madikizela, 1958.

and confined to Johannesburg. Like other leaders and organizers similarly restricted, he continued to work behind the scenes. 'To overthrow oppression,' he said, 'is the highest aspiration of every free man.' And, in a series of hard-hitting articles he analysed the manifold injustices and articulated Black people's demands.

In December 1956 the mammoth Treason Trial of 156 men and women of all races opened. Treason? Much of the evidence was farcical yet had to be seriously dealt with by the distinguished defence team and the accused who, despite the gravity of the charge, were allowed bail. As the years passed, it was a particularly gruelling time for Mandela, Sisulu and their twenty-eight companions who remained in the dock after the case against the others had been dropped.

During the trial Mandela married Winnie Nomzamo Madikizela, a shy and exceptionally lovely young woman from the Transkei who had recently qualified as a medical social worker. (Mandela's earlier marriage, from which he had two sons and a daughter, had ended in divorce.) Winnie not only transformed his small bleak township house, but soon made her own political contribution by joining Albertina Sisulu and hundreds of other women who courted imprisonment when the ANC Women's League protested against the pass laws.

The Treason Trial dragged monotonously on, In December 1960 Mandela gave evidence. Observers from Britain and America had previously thought him an able lawyer and a delightful man; and now, his political maturity was noted, as were the attack of his evidence and the calm authority with which he handled the prosecutor's cross-examination. But they also remarked on a more profound element: a question of growth under challenge. His stature was a measure of the calibre of the ANC's top leadership under its President-General, Albert Lutuli.

The State spent four and a half years trying to prove that the liberation movement was part of an international communist-inspired effort to overthrow the government by violence. When it came

'To overthrow oppression is the highest aspiration of any free man'

Support for the Treason Trial defendants.

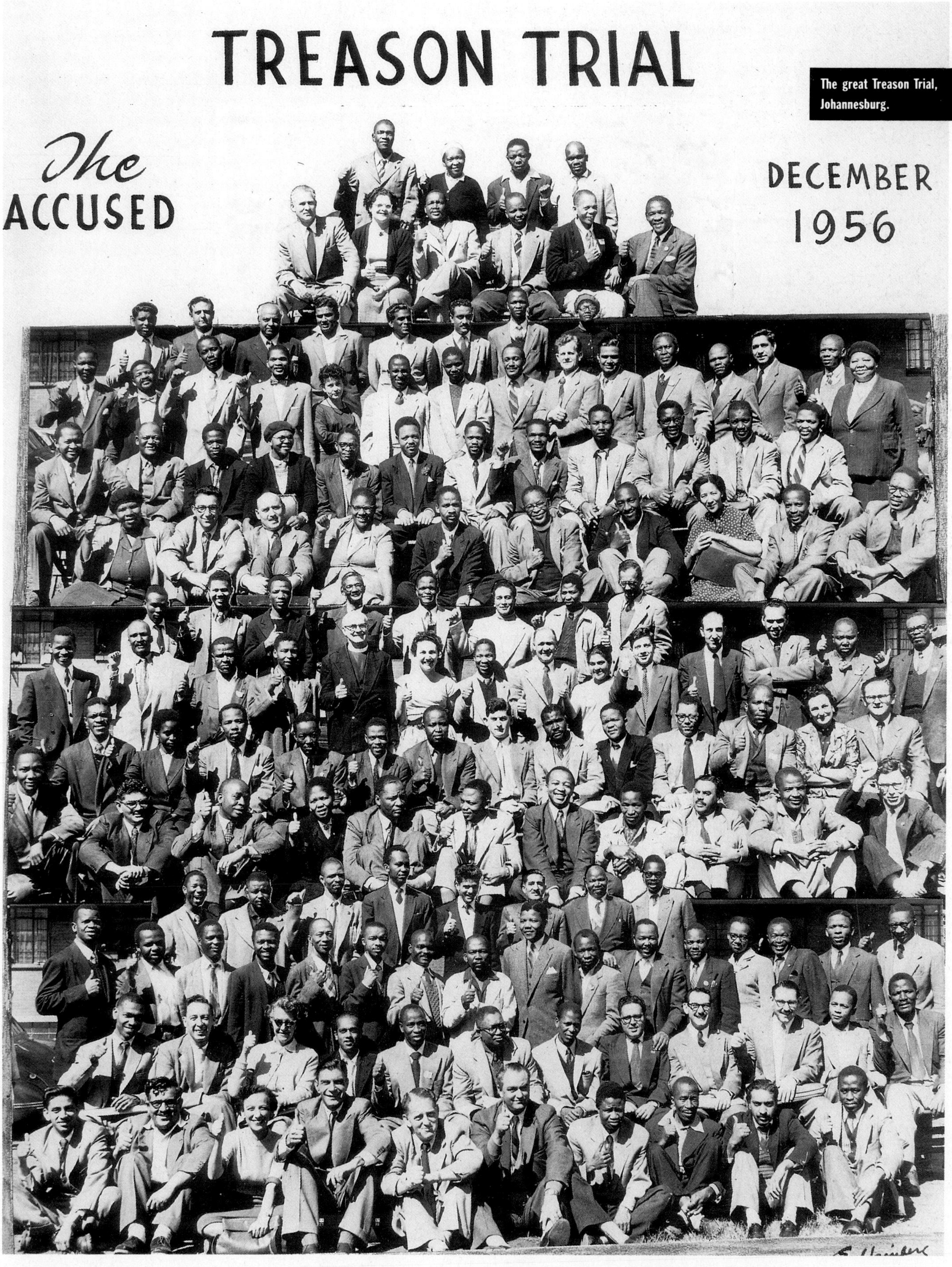
TREASON TRIAL
The ACCUSED
DECEMBER 1956

The great Treason Trial, Johannesburg.

At a township named Sharpeville police shot dead sixty-nine Africans – men, women and children

to judgment, the court found that the ANC and its allies were working 'to replace the present form of State with a radically and fundamentally different form' but that 'violent means' had not been proved. Early in 1961 all the accused were found 'Not Guilty'.

Meanwhile, the violence of the State had been shockingly exposed on 21 March 1960. At a township named Sharpeville, police shot dead sixty-nine Africans – men, women and children – and wounded scores more who had gathered in peaceful protest against the pass laws. Outrage swept the world and in South Africa huge crowds demonstrated their fury. The government declared a State of Emergency. The ANC and the rival Pan Africanist Congress were outlawed; thousands were imprisoned. Emerging from prison, Mandela was deputed by other Black leaders to call for a National Convention to establish a new and democratic South Africa. Should this demand be rejected by the government, he was to organize a countrywide stay-at-home strike.

The government's reaction was to instigate fresh arrests. Mandela went underground. It meant sacrificing his profession and, more importantly, his family life with Winnie and their two small daughters. It was not easy, he said later, 'to say goodbye to the good old days when, at the end of a strenuous day at the office, I could look forward to joining my family at the dinner table, and instead to take up the life of a man hunted continuously by the police . . . . But there comes a time when a man is denied the right to live a normal life, when he can only live the life of an outlaw because the government has so decreed to use the law . . .'. Besides, it was difficult for a well-known public figure, especially so striking a man, to disguise himself. As he daringly eluded the countrywide police search, the press dubbed him the Black Pimpernel.

Celebrating the Treason Trial verdict of 'Not Guilty' (Behind Mandela are Aziz Pahad and Winnie Mandela.

Mandela leads the struggle, 1961.

'There comes a time when a man is denied the right to live a normal life'

'We are striking out along a new road for the liberation of the people'

The strike was met by massive force yet sixty per cent of African labour stayed at home in Johannesburg and Pretoria while in Port Elizabeth seventy-five per cent struck. Mandela, in a secret meeting with British journalists, declared that 'if government reaction is to crush by naked force our non-violent struggle, we will have to seriously reconsider our tactics.' Soberly he added, 'In my mind we are closing a chapter on this question of a non-violent policy.'

Seven months later, in December 1961 that chapter was symbolically closed when Chief Albert Lutuli was awarded the Nobel Prize for Peace in recognition of the ANC's long history of non-violence. Less than a week later, on 16 December, sabotage against symbols of apartheid and government installations marked the birth of Umkhonto we Sizwe, Spear of the Nation. Leaflets proclaimed: 'The time comes in the life of any nation when there remain only two choices: submit or fight. That time has now come to South Africa. We shall not submit .... We are striking out along a new road for the liberation of the people of this country.' While the sabotage continued, Mandela slipped across the border to visit heads of state in Africa, and in London met leaders of the Parliamentary Opposition before embarking on a short course of military training in Algeria. 'Wherever I went,' he said, 'I was treated like a human being.'

Oliver Tambo with Mandela, Addis Ababa 1962.

Mandela in Westminster, 1962.

'Above all Africans want equal rights ... this makes the white man fear democracy'

Soon after returning to South Africa – as so often happens in a police state – he was betrayed by an informer. On 5 August 1962 the Black Pimpernel was captured. Sentenced to five years' hard labour for 'inciting' workers to strike and for leaving the country without valid travel documents, Mandela declared: '. . . when my sentence has been completed, I will still be moved, as men are always moved, by their consciences; I will still be moved ... to take up again, as best I can, the struggle for the removal of injustices until they are finally abolished once and for all.'

Within months he was brought from prison as Accused Number One in the 'Rivonia' Trial. Accused of leading Umkhonto we Sizwe, he did not deny planning sabotage. 'I did not plan it ... because I have any love of violence,' he explained. 'I planned it as a result of a calm and sober assessment of the political situation that had arisen after many years of tyranny, exploitation and oppression of my people by the Whites.'

In the course of a powerful statement which has become an historic document, he declared: 'Above all, Africans want equal political rights .... This makes the White man fear democracy. But this fear cannot be allowed to stand in the way of the only solution which will guarantee racial harmony and freedom for all. It is not true that the enfranchisement of all will result in racial domination .... The ANC has spent half a century fighting against racialism. When it triumphs it will not exchange that policy.... Our struggle is a struggle for the right to live.'

At this point he ceased reading. The court was silent. He looked up at the judge and in a low voice said: 'During my lifetime I have dedicated myself to this struggle of the African people. I have fought against White domination, and I have fought against Black domination. I have cherished the ideal of a democratic and free society in which all persons live together in harmony and with equal opportunities. It is an ideal

'I have cherished the ideal of a democratic and free society'

Mandela's mother and wife arrive at the Palace of Justice for the Rivonia Trial, 1964.

which I hope to live for and to achieve. But if needs be, it is an ideal for which I am prepared to die.'

With his close friend, Walter Sisulu, with Govan Mbeki, Ahmed Kathrada, Raymond Mhlaba, Andrew Mlangeni, Elias Motsoaledi and Dennis Goldberg, in June 1964, he was sentenced to life imprisonment. The *New York Times* said these men were regarded as 'heroes and freedom fighters, the George Washingtons and Benjamin Franklins of South Africa'.

Goldberg, being White, was imprisoned in Pretoria. Mandela, shortly before his forty-sixth birthday, was flown with the other Black defendants to Robben Island, the maximum-security prison on a rocky outcrop surrounded by turbulent seas, seven miles from Cape Town. Police boats patrolled regularly. In any event, during the 400-year history of this notorious island the two or three men who had tried to escape, were drowned in the heavy seas. Mandela and Sisulu were to spend nineteen years there. Oliver Tambo, meanwhile, was leading the struggle from exile.

It was mid-winter, bitterly cold, a foghorn lowing mournfully on days of dense mist. Prison uniform for Africans consisted of shorts and threadbare jerseys. Mandela and his comrades were held in a special section of individual cells with about thirty others. They had to sleep on a concrete floor with a thin mat and only two blankets. There was only cold water to wash in and the food was vile. Nevertheless, Mandela, once a keen amateur boxer, exercised regularly very early each morning. They were allowed one letter every six months – of 500 words, heavily censored if they strayed from family matters – and one visit every six months – of half an hour which was cut short by listening warders if they strayed from family matters. After visits, the men would be quiet and thoughtful, reliving each moment. Then they would share every scrap with each other – Mandela loved to speak of 'Zami'

'It is an ideal for which I am prepared to die'

'Our struggle is a struggle for the right to live'

Zeni and Zindzi
Mandela, at home in
Soweto.

and of her news of Zeni and Zindzi, their two daughters, who would not be allowed to visit him until they reached their teens.

Newspapers were forbidden to the politicals yet somehow they picked up information about events in the outside world.

And all the while, through dank winters and through blazing summers, they laboured with pickaxes and shovels in a lime quarry, day in, day out, year after year after year.

Warders were abusive and quick to punish. But from the start the men had agreed that no matter what they were subjected to, no sign of weakness would be shown. When it came to protesting or making complaints, it was natural that Mandela should represent the section in confronting prison officials. He was not only concerned for his comrades: at a time when 'criminal' prisoners also laboured in the quarry and one was attacked by warders, he intervened to stop the assault, disregarding a warning that it would get him into trouble. 'Our struggle is not just for

ourselves, but for everybody ...' he insisted.

Even men from rival organizations respected, indeed often revered, Mandela and Sisulu. Mandela's interest in people and their experiences, both human and political, was evident in his welcome to newcomers to their section. Nineteen-year-old Salim Essop, brought there after a close friend had dropped to his death from the tenth floor of Security Police headquarters in Johannesburg, and who had himself been badly tortured, derived strength from Mandela, who sat in silence, his hand on Essop's shoulder, as the youth spoke of all he had endured. Another man has said that the government failed dismally in its aims to destroy their morale and to get the world to forget them, 'because being in the company of Mandela and Sisulu, instead of being weakened, they made you strong. Mandela', he added, 'taught me how to survive. When I was ill, he could have asked anybody else to see to me. He came to me personally. He even cleaned my toilet.'

The behaviour of the warders was always unpredictable – suddenly, at night, they might brutally invade the section to search each cell. Solitary confinement on rice water was one punishment. Despite the hardships, the men found cause for laughter, especially at the absurdity of warders

'Mandela taught me how to survive'

Mandela with Walter
Sisulu in the section
yard, Robben Island
1966.

'Our struggle is not for ourselves but for everybody'

and the prison regulations. One day a warder called on all those with driving licences to stand to one side. Thinking they would be given trucks to drive, several of them did so. They were given wheel-barrows to push. They thought it hilarious.

On a memorable day the boilers broke down and the men got no breakfast, no lunch, no supper. All through the day, instead of being marched out to work, they were kept locked in their cells. After furious protests, food was eventually brought into the yard at ten o'clock that night. The cell doors were unlocked but, having arrived in the yard, hungry though they were, the men ignored the food. For the first time in many years they were seeing the night sky, the moon, the Milky Way, the Southern Cross – Mandela, Sisulu, all of them, gazing up and marvelling.

Another 'first' since arriving at the Island was the occasion when they saw children. While labouring in the quarry, they heard childish voices and could see warders' children playing hide-and-seek in nearby bushes. The warder on guard in the quarry started to swear at the children, shouting at them to go away. With one accord the men rounded on him – how dare he behave like that to children!

Meanwhile, the men's protests and their hunger strikes, backed by representations from the outside world, were gradually winning significant improvements in their conditions. These included beds and more edible food, long pants, hot water for wash-ing, and the right to wrap themselves in blankets to keep warm while studying.

For the first time in many years they were seeing the night sky, the moon, the Milky Way, the Southern Cross . . .

The school children of Soweto rebel, June 1976.

Soweto, 1976.

Studies had become a lifeline. Whatever knowledge a man had was shared with the others. Politics was, of course, a popular subject. Mandela taught law while Sisulu was known as a walking encyclopedia on the history of the ANC; Mbeki taught economics, one Indian was an expert on jazz, others on literature. Even while labouring in the quarry they surreptitiously held seminars. One of the worst punishments was to lose the right to study, as happened to Mandela after a newspaper had been found in his cell. He was passionate about the importance of education and, after the uprising of the children of Soweto in 1976, he helped youths sentenced to imprisonment on the Island to continue with their studies.

After the years of the quarry, it was a huge relief to build roads or to collect seaweed for fertilizer from a beach. Back-breaking work, this also had the exhilaration of salt air and tantalizing glimpses of distant ships and of the panorama of Table Mountain looming over Cape Town. The special section now had a communal hall where they ate and played such games as table tennis, scrabble and chess. Govan Mbeki, the eldest of the Rivonia men, learned to play the guitar. Most importantly, during the 1970's, visits and letters were increased to two a month, although some men had no visits at all.

Throughout her husband's long imprisonment on the Island, Winne Mandela was repeatedly banned and arrested. In 1970, after months in solitary confinement during which she was tortured, she was eventually brought to trial with twenty-one others. All were found 'Not Guilty', only to be re-detained under the Terrorism Act and taken back to solitary confinement for further interrogation. Brought to trial again, they were all acquitted. The State – having

Throughout her husband's long imprisonment Winnie Mandela was repeatedly banned and arrested

Winnie Mandela briefly free of bans, addresses the S.A. Black Women's Federation, 1975.

failed even by this drastic persecution to subdue Winnie – in May 1977 banished her to wretched conditions in the inhospitable dorp of Brandfort. Like her husband, she knew that what she suffered was the common lot of innumerable Blacks. She fought back every inch of the way, managing to bring up her two daughters and, after twenty years, emerging triumphant, unbanned and back home in Soweto.

Early in 1982 Mandela, Sisulu, Kathrada, Mhlaba and Mlangeni were abruptly transferred to Pollsmoor maximum-security prison on the mainland. There, isolated from all other prisoners, they were locked in a dormitory cell with its own high-walled yard. Certain conditions were an improvement – the food was better and they could now receive a range of newspapers – but they felt painfully the loss of the communal life in their section on the Island where, freed from labour, they had spent much of the day out of doors. As Mandela later told a visitor, he now knew what Oscar Wilde meant by the 'little tent of blue that prisoners call the sky'.

12 May 1984 proved a momentous day: when Winnie Mandela arrived at Pollsmoor for one of her regular visits, she was given a message from the prison authori-

Senator Edward Kennedy visits Winnie Mandela in her Brandfort exile.

Winnie Mandela's 'home' in Brandfort, 1977.

ties to say that contact visits would now be permitted. For the first time in twenty-two years Nelson and Winnie Mandela were able to embrace.

Through twenty-six years in jail Mandela has remained a free spirit. He is now in a separate cell and apparently spends much of his time reading and studying. Aiming to qualify as an advocate (barrister), he has passed several legal examinations. Despite his age (he was born on 18 July 1918), he has kept tremendously fit and, according to a recent visitor, bears no resemblence to most portraits: white-haired, tall and upright as ever, he is slim and looks remarkably youthful. After three meetings with him in 1986, the Common-wealth Group said: 'We were first struck by his physical authority – by his immaculate appearance, his apparent good health and his commanding presence. In his manner he exuded authority and received the respect of all around him, including his gaolers . . . . Our final impression was of a man who yearned for his freedom and who longed to be reunited with his family, but

For the first time in twenty-two years Nelson and Winnie Mandela were able to embrace

Zindzi Mandela reads a statement from her father refusing a conditional release from life sentence, Jabulani Stadium, 1985.

‘He longed to be allowed to contribute to the process of reconciliation’

who would never accept it under what he called "humiliating conditions" . . . . We found him unmarked by any trace of bitterness despite his long imprisonment. His over-riding concern was for the welfare of all races in South Africa in a just society; he longed to be allowed to contribute to the process of reconciliation.'*

In a country racked by racial unrest, the government's only response has been to impose increasingly savage States of Emergency, partially disguised by rigid censorship. The ever-rising death toll includes hundreds of children and it is estimated that a third of the 30,000 detainees held since 1986 have been children, many of whom were tortured. More than 1,000 people are still held. A number of community leaders have been assassinated and the conditions created for so-called Black-on-Black violence. Meanwhile demands for Mandela's release have intensified. What an atrocious, tragic waste for South Africa – for Whites as well as Blacks – that his wisdom and strength, his generosity and humour, have not been used in leading that country towards a just society.

In January 1985 President Botha announced that Nelson Mandela could be released; all he had to do was to renounce violence. Mandela's reply, addressed to his people, was uncompromising. He pointed out that only when all other forms of resistance had been crushed by the State, had Blacks turned to armed struggle. 'Let *him* [Botha] renounce violence,' he concluded. 'Let him say that he will dismantle apartheid . . . . I cannot and will not give any undertaking at a time when I and you, the people, are not free. Your freedom and mine cannot be separated. I will return.'

MARY BENSON

'Your freedom and mine cannot be separated. I will return'

Mission to South Africa, Penguin, 1986

THE DAY

It was a day to top all days. A day of hope and optimism. In sixty countries, all over the world, from Russia and the Eastern Block to Australia and New Zealand, from the United States to the Middle East, from Brazil to Africa, we the privileged, the favoured children of the world paused for a moment in our endless getting and spending and thought of those less free.

11 June, Wembley Stadium, London, the Nelson Mandela 70th Birthday Tribute Concert. After a year of thought and organization the scale of which must be likened to marshalling forces for a military invasion, up to half a billion people around the world were treated to a day of tightly programmed performances from such as the Eurythmics, Chrissie Hynde and UB40, George Michael, Sly and Robbie, the incandescent Whitney Houston who backed a gospel tune sang by her mother, Cissy, Dire Straits with Eric Clapton, Al Green, Roberta Flack and Natalie Cole. Chubby Checker and The Fat Boys set the stadium twisting, Phil Collins played in Midge Ure's super group. Simple Minds and Jim Kerr played a full set of their ecstatic music, the notes of Peter Gabriel's 'Biko' soared through the air with Youssou N'Dour's accompaniment. The glorious Stevie Wonder sang – and the world sang with him – 'I just called to say I love you'. It was a day of fanatastic music, set into a magnificently planned production, paying tribute to one of the world's most courageous men and the cause he symbolizes.

There was some small heroism and sacrifice involved by everyone. The crowds in the stadium stood grinning and clapping, shouting and singing kneedeep in fast food wrappers and mud for ten hours without complaint. Scotland Yard reported there were a surprising lack of incidents for an assembly of this size. The spirit touched everyone involved. Artists had rescheduled their tours to be present, some had flown in especially for the concert. George Michael sang a version of Marvin Gaye's 'Sexual Healing', defying doctor's orders who had said he would jeopardise his world tour by singing twice in one day. Sting said 'nothing could have stopped me being here' and left the stage, tears in his eyes, saying that 'this is the most emotional experience of my life'. Bands had rehearsed for up to three weeks especially for the concert to maintain the high production values demanded by the organizers, choosing songs that they thought would particularly pay tribute to Mandela. Many of the workers on the project were paid half of their usual fee, many volunteered their services.

Harry Belafonte, the most articulate and gentle speaker of all the musicians, cried out that 'Mandela was the leader of South Africa's oppressed black people' and 'a symbol of the fight against the cruel and unjust system of apartheid.' Annie Lennox ended a song crying out for the release of all political prisoners and led the crowd in a chant of 'Freedom to South Africa'. Whitney Houston cried, 'You know we could have been anywhere else in the world we wanted to be tonight, but we're not. We're here to celebrate Nelson Mandela's birthday.'

Stevie Wonder, the surprise guest of the show sang two songs and said in the clearest statement of the day 'Nelson Mandela, this day we are very conscious of the fact that you are not free, we are very conscious of the fact that till you are free, no man, woman or child, of whatever culture or colour is truly free. Till the world wakes up, till we as a unity of human people of all cultures come together and realize that oppression of anyone is oppression of everyone, we will never be free.'

Nor was this a concert of one superstar group after another. Some of the unsung heroes of the music world performed in unique combinations. They too made their contribution, reminding us of the giant wellspring of talent in all of us. Dance groups like Amampondo from the townships of South Africa and the Experimental Dance Troupe from Angola entertained on the satellite stage, comedians Lenny Henry, Graham Chapman and Michael Palin from Monty Python and Whoopi Goldberg made us laugh. Actors and actresses like Richard Gere, Ali McGraw, Daryl Hannah, Denzel Washington and Gregory Hines introduced the acts. Sir Richard Attenborough made an appearance. Jessye Norman, the superstar operatic soprano closed the concert with 'Amazing Grace'.

At the same time we had the satisfaction of participating in one of the most ordered events of this kind. We had learned a lot from Live Aid. Seventy-two thousand watched three hundred performers while thousands of backstage workers, technicians, photographers, journalists, television producers, promoters and managers brought that experience to sixty countries and an estimated half a billion viewers. It went smoothly. No ratcheting, no backstage tantrums, no hitches that weren't solved, just a long ten hours of blissful, elegaic music from all over the world. World music and global pop. The world was tapping its foot and humming.

There was much talk of what a concert like this could actually do. What effect it could actually have. There were no pleas for money. There was nothing we could actually do. Just bear witness, pay tribute to the man who symbolizes the fight against apartheid. And in that stood the most moving moments of the concert. The simple chorus of 'Happy Birthday' started and sung by the audience as they filed out. The simple hope expressed by all the stars, musicians and organisers that those watching would be more aware of the situation in South Africa. Few people at Wembley on 11 June had a political axe to grind. Few knew enough about the situation in South Africa to have a profoundly educated conversation. That was not the point. The actual ramifications on South Africa of Mandela's release was beyond the knowledge of most of us. That didn't matter. One thing we knew to the very depths of our souls was that the system of apartheid is wrong, evil and dangerous. That it chokes and destroys the lives of millions. That it is a cancer on the continent of Africa and we too called for its end.

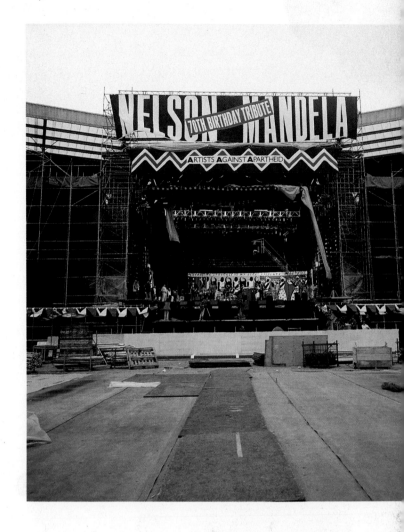

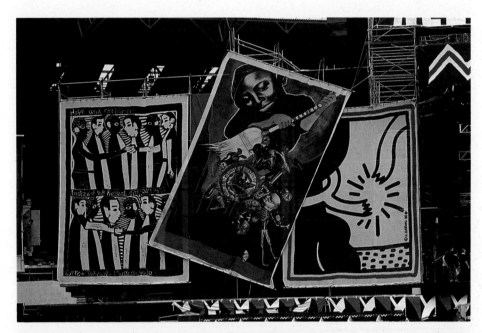

Special stage artwork by, left to right, John Muafangejo Hope And Optimism, *Sue Coe* A Clean Sweep *and Keith Haring* Untitled

Artwork by, left to right, Keith Haring Untitled, *Ralph Steadman* The Stuggle Is My Life *and John Muafangejo* Hope And Optimism

The Eyes of The World *painted by Malangatana Ngwenya*

Loadsa
Freedom…comedian
Harry Enfield

White & Black & Green…Daryl Hannah with Al Green

A cross-cultural reference for Annie Lennox

Salad days for The Fat Boys

Smiling for Nelson...Salt 'n' Pepa

L.A. Law's Corbin Bernsen enjoys the spectacle of actress Jennifer Beals

Hi tech, low tension for Spandau Ballet's Tony Hadley

A new power trio…Chubby Checker, Archbishop Trevor Huddleston and Harry Belafonte

Cole mining…Bryan Adams and Natalie Cole

Little And Large…Little Steven with The Fat Boys

'As a representative of your Government…'
Michael Palin

Sting and Mike

Jim Kerr and Mike

Whoopi Goldberg and Mike

Stevie Wonder interviewed by Paul Gambaccini

Neil and Glenys Kinnock: solidarity with Nelson Mandela

Soul summit…Joe Cocker and Stevie Wonder

Little Steven talks to Harry Belafonte

Harry Belafonte interviewed by Paul Gambaccini

Harry Belafonte listens to Ali McGraw

SET THEM FREE

On the stage are five giant blowups of art works contributed by Keith Herring, Ralph Steadman, Sue Coe, John Muafangejo, and Malangatana Valente Mgwenya. 'Free Nelson Mandela' hangs over the stage and a banner 'Artists Against Apartheid' hangs over the band. Five backdrops will interchange with each other throughout the day. At the beginning, and strikingly, is a black and white blow up of Mandela's face.

The day begins with power. Sting, George Michael, the Eurythmics. Three powerhouses of talent and inspiration. It is a magnificent kick off.

'My contribution, and everyone else's contribution is a small thing, but it's cumulative. It's actually really about raising people's awareness of the situation. You saw that after Live Aid there was a tremendous tidal wave of people becoming much more aware about world affairs. If we can change people's opinions slowly, if we can make them aware of what's going on, then I think this concert has achieved a great deal.' – Annie Lennox

It was this attitude that shone through the day. Every artist and every backstage worker, every member of the audience agreed with Lennox. She continued. 'Well, you know, I'm not really a politician or an expert on this. All I know is that morally I entirely disagree with the prospect of apartheid.'

None could quarrel. But it was in the music that most of the artists made their point. Cast in this light, sting's 'Set Them Free' became a poignant anthem and 'Every Step You Take' became threatening, redolent of the atmosphere of South Africa. The Eurythmics 'You Could Have Placed a Chill in My Heart' could have been dedicated to Botha and the crowd singing along with Annie Lennox in 'Sweet Dreams' indicated our mass hope for tomorrow.

George Michael, who confined his songs entirely to those composed by black musicians, said that he wanted to demonstrate the depth of his and our debt to black music. 'We all know that we're here for,' he said, before breaking into his first song. He began with Stevie Wonder's 'Village Ghetto-land', sang a haunting 'If You Were My Woman', and ended with Marvin Gaye's 'Sexual Healing'.

The Eurythmics set returned us to full power rock and roll, 1988. The crowd was swept away by Dave Stewart and Annie Lennox's production and commitment. It was here that the organizers request that each band be fully rehearsed began to pay off. Each set was like a mini concert, abstracted from one of their best tours. But with a committed stance. Each song was chosen carefully, each song introduced with care and meaning. Annie Lennox, pale and wreathed in smiles, altered some of the words to 'When Tomorrow Comes' and sang 'When tomorrow comes there will be no more apartheid in this world'. 'It's a Brand New Day' was dedicated to Nelson Mandela and introduced by a shout of 'Well, hey Mandela! We want freedom in South Africa!! Happy Birthday to you!!!'

'We are here today, all of us, 72,000 in the Stadium and millions more viewing in sixty countries across the world. We are here to take part in a unique thing, to honour a great man, a man who is the leader of South Africa's oppressed black people.'

'He is a symbol of their fight against the cruel and unjust system of apartheid. He has been a prisoner, locked up for twenty-five years in a South African prison. He languishes there for his belief that his people should be free. The man is Nelson Mandela.'

'Today we celebrate his 70th birthday. Our celebration today is the most spectacular rock concert since Live Aid. For the next ten and a half hours you will hear rock, pop and jazz, rhythm and blues . . . great music of every kind. But the message behind all of it is quite simple. We salute you Nelson Mandela and we want to see you and your fellow political prisoners free.'
HARRY BELAFONTE

Harry Belafonte: 'We salute you Nelson Mandela'

Lenny Henry keeps in trim for the Mandela Marathon

'There's gonna be ten solid hours of music, dance and comedy . . . and that's just me!' LENNY HENRY

Compere Lenny Henry

Africa's Farafina

STING

Sting's backing singer Dolette McDonald

Sting's massed ensemble

Sting

'To anyone who
objects to apartheid
Nelson Mandela
stands for protest
against apartheid.
Twenty-five years is
a long time.'
GEORGE MICHAEL

Sir Richard Attenborough

'We are all here this afternoon to honour a very remarkable man, a man of unshakeable principle and extraordinary courage and I feel very privileged to be amongst those paying tribute to him.'

SIR RICHARD ATTENBOROUGH

South Africa's Amampondo

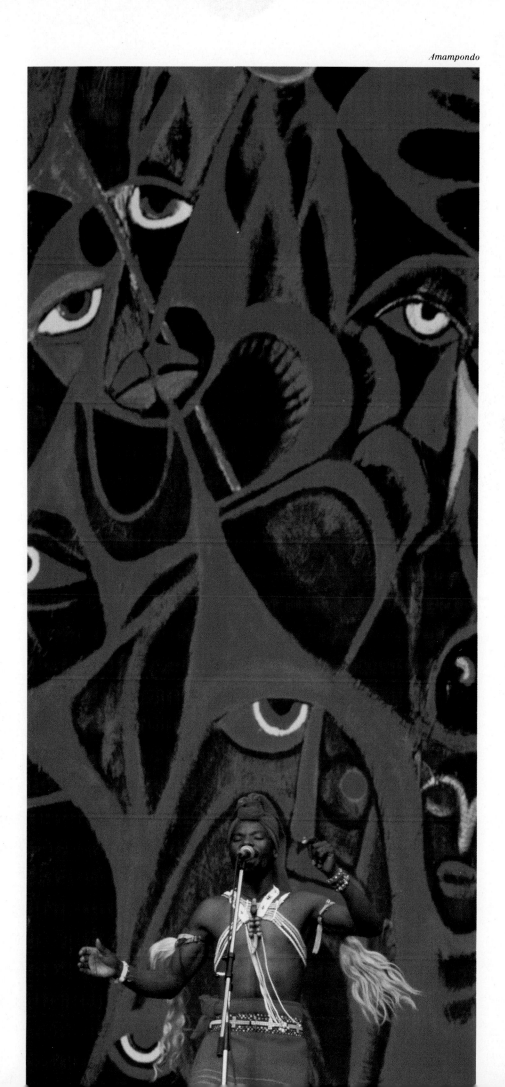

Annie Lennox

*The Dervish
dance...Annie Lennox
with The Eurythmics'
backing singer Joniece
Jamieson*

'Change is never something that will happen very quickly, or overnight, and Mandela knows that only too well. He's been in prison for twenty-six years. My contribution, and everyone else's contribution, is a small thing but it's cumulative. It's actually really about raising people's awareness of the situation and you saw that after Live Aid there was a tremendous tidal wave of people becoming much more aware about world affairs. If we can change people's opinions slowly, if we can make them aware of what's going on, then I think this concert has achieved a great deal. It's already achieving a great deal.' ANNIE LENNOX: EURYTHMICS

Dave Stewart

'Hey Mandela
We want freedom in South Africa
I said hey Mandela Happy Birthday to you!'
EURYTHMICS

Annie Lennox

Amabutho

Lenny 'Michael Jackson' Henry

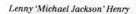

'I love you so much. Bubbles loves you, Bubbles my pet chimpanzee loves you. Do you love Bubbles?' LENNY HENRY AS MICHAEL JACKSON

UNCHAIN MY HEART

T he sheer musical variety of the concert was something stagger-ing. The Arnhem Land Dance Troupe from Australia bounced off jazz musicians and American nighttime soap stars. There was humour from Lenny Henry and Whoopi Goldberg, ex Monty Pythonites Graham Chapman and Michael Palin, intros from romantic idols Richard Gere and Daryl Hannah. Folk music from Tracy Chapman. Rap from The Fat Boys. 'Amazing Grace' from Jessye Norman. Truly creative programming.

Offbeat musical juxapositions were the best surprises of the day. For not only were we treated to some of the best performing acts in the world, we also saw the musicians working together almost privately, as they would wish they could, with their favourites, their heroes, the admired collea-gues. As Natalie Cole said when asked how she liked the concert, 'Well you know, I was working with great, great people ... we had a ball.'

The Soul Revue with the Reverend Al Green, Joe Cocker, Freddie Jackson, Ashford and Simpson and Natalie Cole led off from with the gently sad sounds of the American South, the roots of rock and roll, sweet soul music.

'Lets Stay Together' by seven-time Grammy Award Winner, Al Green. Uneven and hitting a few wrong notes but he still managed to deliver a song like no other soul singer can, stripped of computer styl-ing, deep down, real life, true soul.

'From all over the world, Mr Mandela, next year we want you here to party' went the intro and Mr Joe Cocker the man with that unquenchable wild glint in his eye, sang 'Unchain My Heart'.

References to South Africa were muted in this set. 'Welcome to the world and that means South Africa.' 'I dedicate this song to Nelson Mandela', said Jonathon Butler, introducing his song, 'True Love Never Fails'. Freddie Jackson simply wanted to 'Jam Tonight', Ashford and Simpson's 'message was in the song', 'Ain't No Moun-tain High Enough'. Natalie Cole sang her hit 'Pink Cadillac'. Pure fun. The set ended with the classic 'He's Got the Whole World in His Hands'. The roots of American soul.

For the Stadium, the real spirit of the occasion could be found. The 70,000-strong crowd were for the most part, young and unanimously cheerful. Standing for hours in the grey light of an English summer, kneedeep in wrappers and beer cans, mud and grime, they were invariably enthu-siastic. Vox pop interviews conducted among them early in the day had revealed that the majority had been attracted by the musical talent, rather than the message the talent was endorsing. As the day wore on, that feeling began to change.

The Reverend Al Green

'We are here . . . to enhance the freedom of Mr Mandela and his cause, for peace and justice around the world. Not only in South Africa but around the world, for all people.'

AL GREEN

Sheffield steel...Joe Cocker

'When I was offered to do this I felt honoured, especially to be sandwiched in between all those great black artists too . . .' JOE COCKER

Jonathon Butler

Freddie Jackson

Natalie Cole

'We want to do
something that will
give us even more
of a feeling of unity
and that's what
we're all here for
and that, in spite of
the way things look
today, Nelson
Mandela we love
you . . .' NATALIE COLE

Natalie Cole

Soul giants Ashford And Simpson

'The message is in the music. We hope these
words say just how badly we wanted to be here...'
VALERIE SIMPSON

The soul finale… left to
right, Freddie Jackson,
Natalie Cole, musical
arranger HB Barnum,
Joe Cocker, Al Green,
Ashford And Simpson
and Jonathan Butler

America's finest young
folk singer Tracey
Chapman

Wet Wet Wet

HARVEST
FOR THE WORLD

I f it were possible to make a dream list for the world then ending apartheid would be on it. In this concert several hundred million dreamt this dream. How could this not be a powerful force?

Daryl Hannah, long blond hair streaming, came on to introduce the Midge Ure super group and said simply that this day was also the twenty-fifth anniversary of white schools in the states being forced to accept black students.

The Midge Ure section of the show featured such stellar names as Phil Collins, Steve Norman and Tony Hadley from Spandau Ballet, one of America's greatest saxophonists David Sanborn, drummer Mark Brzezicki from Big Country, Paul Young, Paul Carrack (singing 'How Long', the smash hit from his days with Ace), the glorious Joan Armatrading, Mick Karn, Marillion's Mark Kelly and Fish and Wet Wet Wet.

Curt Smith from Tears For Fears sang 'Everybody Wants To Rule The World' and got the crowd bouncing in nostalgia for one of the best songs of 1985. Bryan Adams from Canada sang a simple song with the simple message of needing somebody like you. The Bee Gees closed the set.

Midge Ure's song was the most direct. The lyrics dared to dream the dream.
'Dear God
Give me love for the lonely
Give me food for the hungry
Give me peace in our restless world
Give me hope for the children
Give me a worldwide religion.'

American actress Daryl Hannah introduces Midge Ure's Allstars

'Today is also the twenty-fifth anniversary of the day that white schools in America were forced by law to admit black students.'
DARYL HANNAH

Steve Norman

Midge Ure

Paul Carrack performing with Midge Ure's Allstars

Fish from Marillion

STEVE NORMAN
MIDGE URE
PAUL CARRACK
FISH

Bryan Adams

Phil Collins

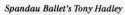

Spandau Ballet's Tony Hadley

Joan Armatrading

Paul Young

Tears For Fears' Curt Smith

CURT SMITH

Maurice, Robin and Barry…the Bee Gees

AFRICAN REGGAE
YEAH!

One of the great achievments of the Nelson Mandela Birthday Tribute Concert was that it brought indigenous African music and great singers such as Salif Keita and Youssou N'Dour to the attention of the Wembley audience .

Sly and Robbie were joined by Salif and Youssou to form one band. Philip Michael Thomas from *Miami Vice* and Ali McGraw introduced Jonas Gwangwa, the award winning composer of 'Cry Freedom'. Gwangwa brought South Africa to the stage with a band and dancers. Salif Keita from Mali and Youssou N'Dour from Senegal are two of the world's great singers. they brought the special African interplay of instrument and voice to a pop concert. Voice and rhythm dominate melody – and the driven quality of much of Western music is diminished. Something to learn.

Youssou N'Dour's soaring voice silenced the crowd. Aswad, Britain's favourite reggae band, played with that quintessential Wyoming cowboy, Jackson Browne who sang of freedom, of walls crumbling and stones turning. Aswad started all the artists singing, beginning with a shout: 'We believe each and every person has an equal right!' On stage poured reggae stars Maxi Priest and Barrington Levy together with Marti Pellow from Wet Wet Wet, Harry Bowens from Was (Not Was) and Peter Gabriel to join the chorus of 'Set Them Free'.

The seriousness of the Mahotella Queens, from the townships of South Africa, in grass skirts, head dresses and lots of great jewellery, stirred up the hearts. These were new sound combinations to many of us. Filter down they must, entering the ever-widening vocabulary of music.

The crowd was seduced by the sounds of Africa. It was impossible not to fall a bit in love with these people through their music, its joy, variety, fun and humanity. It was half time. The afternoon was waning. The supergroups were on their way.

Jonas Gwangwa's African chorus

'... and I come here to praise Mandela
And to bring this message to his jailer
Your walls may hold the man inside
But you'll never hold back the human tide.'
– When the Stone Begins to Turn JACKSON BROWNE

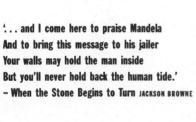

JACKSON BROWNE

Drummie Zeb, Brinsley Forde and Tony Gad....Aswad

Jackson Browne, Peter Gabriel and Youssou N'Dour

RAY LEMA

Ray Lema from Zaire

Jamaica's finest bassist...Robbie Shakespeare

African superstar Salif Keita

'We believe each and
every person
deserves an equal
right. Unity is
strength.'
BRINSLEY FORDE, ASWAD

Left to right, Youssou N'Dour, Jackson Browne, Robbie Shakespeare, and Salif Keita

'Now you can fool some of the people some of the time
But you can't fool all the people all the time
Those who invest in Botha's regime
Yes, they are living the apartheid dream.'
– Set Them Free ASWAD

Aswad with Marti from Wet Wet Wet…'Set them free!'

Solidarity. Left to right Djene Doumbouya, Salif Keita, Jackson Browne, Peter Gabriel, Youssou N'Dour and, from Was (Not Was), Harry Bowens

BRING BACK
NELSON MANDELA

By this time in the concert the sweat of late afternoon had drenched us, the rhythm of South Africa had warmed us and we were about to be treated to the Birmingham reggae sound of UB40.

Appropriately enough 'There's a Rat in the Kitchen' opened the set, followed by the song 'Red Red Wine' which got the entire Stadium to its feet. Chrissie Hynde came on stage to sing duets of 'You Get Me Babe' and 'Breakfast in Bed'. On the video monitors were photos and family film of Winnie and Nelson Mandela.

The set ended with 'We will fight for the right to be free, we will build our own society. We will sing our own song.' The lyric, repeated over and over brought Lenny Henry and Richard Gere out on stage to sing the chorus over and over again. 'Amanda Ngawethu!'

Gere then made a moving plea in his introduction to Hugh Masekela and Miriam Makeba. 'Nelson is having his birthday in his cell. I think about the tremendous energy being generated out of this event. You know one of the things about South Africa is that the black man has no right of representation. We do! It is our responsibility to use that power!'

Whoopi Goldberg joined in the sentiment. 'Everytime they look at these faces out here, they know apartheid is wrong! Everytime they look at the stage, they see whose name?' Then she led the crowd in a massive shout, yelling five times 'how long?'

Hugh Masekala and Miriam Makeba were up next. Masekala's trumpet had a clarion sound to it. Jazz fusion, R and B rhythm, lots of funk. Masekela had a gravity on stage, brought by his stature as elder statesman of South African music. He sang and played a haunting song to the men of South Africa, brought in by train from all over Southern Africa to work in the gold mines of Johannesburg. His whole band joined in a song called 'Free Nelson Mandela'. 'Bring back Nelson Mandela,' went the lyrics. 'Free Mandela, bring him back to Soweto. I want to see him walking down the avenue with Winnie Mandela.'

Miriam Makeba, resplendent in a commanding version of ethnic dress, lent the concert a kind of credibility, a connection with the country to whose pain we were paying our respects. Her music and voice connected us to the courage and strength of the women of South Africa.

Masekela and Makeba are long time freedom fighters, leaving South Africa over twenty years ago, to work in the freer atmosphere of the United States, developing the glorious talents in a friendly climate, living slow, painful, frustrating years trying to awaken the world to South Africa. Being here, on this day, was for them a great reward, a milestone on their long path towards freedom for their countrymen.

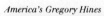

America's Gregory Hines

'We hope that next year when we come together to celebrate again Mr Mandela will be here with us in person.'
GREGORY HINES

UB40's Ali Campbell

'There are 750 million people watching this concert around the world in sixty-four different countries and it's ironic that the one country that wants to hear what we have to say is not listening. And that's South Africa.'
ROBIN CAMPBELL, UB40

'This next song is about South Africa and it's not only dedicated to Nelson Mandela but also to Winnie Mandela who keeps on the struggle while he's inside, Steve Biko and all the countless thousands who've died in South Africa in the struggle to rid South Africa of the cancer of apartheid. It's also dedicated in support of the ANC and SWAPO . . .' ROBIN CAMPBELL, UB40

UB40's Brian Travers

Pretender Chrissie Hynde with UB40's Ali Campbell

'I Got You Babe...'

'It's an amazing event and I think the extraordinary thing is that all this energy is generated from one man that none of us has ever met. Nelson Mandela. I think it's an extraordinary lesson about the power of goodness, and the power of the individual, motivated by goodness and compassion and ultruism, can affect the entire planet.'
RICHARD GERE

Richard Gere

Whoopi Goldberg

'Fear makes people write letters and say that concerts like this are offensive. But isn't it true that the offence is that they would try to keep you from seeing people you like? And isn't it true that no matter what the South African Consulate says, no matter what Mrs Thatcher says, the fact of the matter is that apartheid is wrong and everytime they look at these faces out here they know apartheid is wrong.'
WHOOPI GOLDBERG

WHOOPI GOLDBERG

Miriam Makeba

Hugh Masekela

AIN'T GONNA PLAY SUN CITY

Jim Kerr and Simple Minds came on to the single pulsing note of the bass against the backdrop of black faces. 'For Nelson Mandela' shouted Kerr. 'and for the people of South Africa who only want a part of what is naturally theirs.' and the band kicked into 'Walk Away'.

Joined for the second song by Johnny Marr, late of The Smiths, they played what Kerr called a 30 year old American protest song, 'Summertime Blues'.

Kerr introduced the next song, 'Mandela Day' by saying that the band was merely representing all people, people from his home town, ordinary people, people in all countries all over the world and dedicated the song to all the people in South Africa who have given their lives to the struggle. 'May they rest in peace!' he called. One line echoed the hope, 'Freedom moves in closer every day.'

Perhaps this was the most politicized set of the concert. 'Alive and Kicking' was dedicated to all the people in the townships. Each song had its inherent meaning borrowed for the occasion, yet Kerr and Simple Minds did what they always managed to do, that is, put the audience in touch with their spiritual selves, and the energy of those selves. The faces of the audience were lit up, generous, smiling, transformed.

Peter Gabriel came on with Youssou N'Dour and introduced his songs with the words 'South Africa is the only country in the world that has racism enshrined in its constitution. This is a message from all of us, and all of you to the sons and daughters of the South African Government. It is time for a change.' The haunting notes of 'Biko' floated over our heads. 'You can blow out a candle, but you can't blow out a fire.'

The rest of the set became one long anthem for freedom. Jim Kerr introduced the next guest with the words, 'One man had the courage to go to South Africa and see for himself what was going on. Out of that came one of the best pop songs ever written, 'Ain't Going To Play Sun City'. A resounding cheer. Out came Little Steven, Steven Van Zandt, who likewise called Jackson Browne, Youssou N'Dour, Daryl Hannah, Peter Gabriel and Meatloaf on stage as backup singers. Said Little Steven to the audience, 'You could have stayed home – you didn't. You came to send a message. People watching TV – you could be watching something else. You aren't – you are watching to send a message. We have been quiet too long, we have been patient too long. We the people demand the unconditional release of Nelson Mandela.'

An equally ecstatic reception greeted Jerry Dammers, founder of 'Artists Against Apartheid' and inspirational force behind the Nelson Mandela tribute. Dammers is the composer of the song, 'Free Nelson Mandela'. Half the South African performers at the concert joined him on stage.

This set was one of high seriousness. The audience watched as performer after performer demonstrated his or her loyalty and commitment to the humanitarian cause of freedom and the end of apartheid.

Britain's IDJ jazz dancers

Britain's supreme jazz saxophonist Courtney Pine

Simple Minds

Peter Gabriel and Jim Kerr

'South Africa is the only country in the world that has racism enshrined in its Constitution. It's a message from all of us and all of you to the sons and daughters of the South African Government that it's time for a change.'
PETER GABRIEL

Simple Minds' Jim Kerr

SIMPLE MINDS

Simple Minds' Jim Kerr

'Ain't gonna play Sun City…' Little Steven and Jim Kerr

'We've been quiet too long, we've been patient too long. We the people will no longer tolerate the terrorism of the Government of South Africa. We will no longer do business with those who do business with the terrorist Government of South Africa. We will no longer vote for politicians who refuse to enforce the economic boycott of the terrorist Government of South Africa. Most of all, we the people demand the unconditional release of Nelson Mandela.' LITTLE STEVEN

Left to right Meatloaf, Daryl Hannah, Jackson Browne, Peter Gabriel and Youssou N'Dour

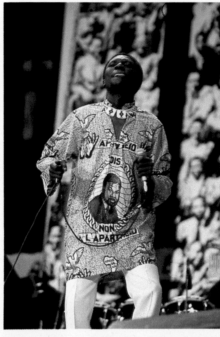

The Jerry Dammers group with Frank Williams (saxophone), Dick Cuthell (trumpet), David de Fries (trumpet) and Jonas Gwangwa (trombone) together with an African chorus

Ndanda Khuze from the Amandla Cultural Troupe of the ANC... and lead singer on 'Free Nelson Mandela'

'Free Nelson Mandela!'

I JUST CALLED TO SAY I LOVE YOU

Dark had fallen. UB40 and Simple Minds had fired the imagination of the crowd and there was much shouting and cheering when Mandela's name was mentioned. By the time Stevie Wonder and Whitney Houston took the stage the concert had long become a celebration of humanity and hope for the future. Wonder, whose software had been stolen, was delayed briefly, but when he came on, his message was so pure and warm, his music so beautiful, the audience had a collective lump in its throat.

Whitney Houston broke her world tour to appear at the Nelson Mandela Tribute. Whitney began every song with a reference to Mandela. 'Oh, it's a real real pleasure for ne to be here to night.' she said. And we believed her. 'Aren't you glad you're here?' she shouted and the crowd yelled 'Yess!!!' in deafening tones. 'This one's for Nelson Mandela, this one's from me to you, Nelson …' And she broke into a gospel treatment of 'Where Do Broken Hearts Go?'

The set continued in this vein, Whitney shouting her tribute and love for a man she had never seen and the crowd yelling along with her. 'Happy Birthday Nelson Mandela!!! Nelson will save the day! He will, I know he will!' went the introduction to 'Love Will Save The Day'. Whitney's mother, Cissie, joined her sang a classic gospel song of invocation. 'He can turn the tide. I know he will. I believe that someone's hearing every word.' went the lyrics. Whitney has the entire arena and probably half the television audience dancing to 'I Wanna Dance With Somebody' and dedicated 'The Greatest Love' to 'Nelson Mandela and his family and to all my South African brothers and sisters.'

At the end of this set, Meatloaf came on stage, screamed 'God bless you' and introduced Salt'n'Pepa, the girl rap group who 'wanted everybody to jump for Nelson Mandela.'

The rap section was indicative of the imaginative programming of the concert. Performances on the satellite stage accounted for two and a half hours of the production, 25 per cent of the whole show. Rap, comedy, folk songs and dance went out to an audience far greater than ever before. Derek B., The Fat Boys, Chubby Checker made us dance.

Stevie, who sang the classic 'I Just Called To Say I Love You', had the stadium singing along with him spontaneously. The heart of Stevie Wonder is so pure that everyone who came in contact with him remarked how warmly they felt about him. He gave so much of himself on stage that we as an audience believed in him. He danced and jumped around so much, he was literally pulled back from the edge of the stage by his musicians.

'You know', he said backstage earlier, 'the artist is just a reflection of other people who are expressing these feelings … we want oppression in South Africa done away with. It's brutal, it's ignorance and it's as simple as that.'

Whitney Houston

Whitney Houston with her mother Cissy

'One courageous
individual has been
imprisoned for so
long and taken away
from his family. It's
important we realise
this.' WHITNEY HOUSTON

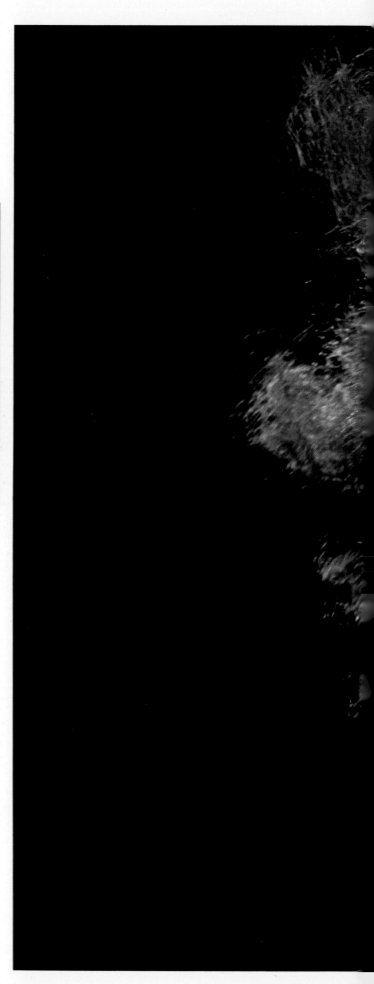

'We just called to say Happy Birthday Nelson Mandela
We just called to say we love you
And we mean it from the bottom of our hearts.'

'Nelson Mandela . . . we are all very conscious of
the fact that until you are free no man, woman
or child, whatever their colour or culture they
come from, is really free . . . oppression of
anyone is oppression of everyone.' STEVIE WONDER

The even bigger Fat Boys

Chubby Checker

BROTHERS IN ARMS

Scottish comedian Billy Connolly introduced Dire Straits by telling the story of the South African proceeds to their first album. The band had asked that all proceeds be donated to Amnesty International. Connolly commented that the thought of South Africans every year since 1979 making out a cheque to Amnesty International gave him much pleasure. The band has been banned in South Africa since that time.

'This is the reason we got the band back together.' shouted Mark Knopfler and the band broke into 'Do The Walk On By'. An hour long set of Dire Straits' controlled virtuosity soothed the fevers of the audience and their sweet seriousness captured out hearts. The audience swayed back and forth to the tunes, danced to 'Sultans of Swing' and sang softly along to 'Julia'. The music of country bars had come to Wembley, with all its classic rock and roll, its depth of feeling.

'This song is for the gentleman in question', shouted Mark Knopfler, 'This is the best birthday party we've ever been to.' And Dire Straits broke into 'One Humanity One

Justice'. The message was in the music, as it had been throughout the day. In the humanity of music, in its power to provoke sympathy, in its language of universality.

Eric Clapton sang 'You Were Wonderful Tonight' and his cool adept hand with a guitar throughout the hour provided an extra dimension to the set.

After a full hour of Dire Straits the band left the stage to tumultuous applause. There was a pause, and Jessye Norman, the world famous soprano took command of the stage. The notes of 'Amazing Grace' resounded through the arena, broken only during the pauses by shouts of appreciation. The final notes faded. The crowd roared for the last time. Candles were lit and fireworks surrounded the perimeter.

Slowly the audience began filing out. It had been a long day, replete with emotion and pleasure and for many, learning. We had paid tribute to a man far away who had proved to us the humanity, the possibility of courage and self sacrifice that is present in all of us. Slowly, quietly, the song began and the departing audience sang happy birthday one last time to Nelson Mandela.

Billy Connolly

DIRE STRAITS

*Dire Straits with special
guest Eric Clapton*

Dire Straits' Mark Knopfler

Eric Clapton

Eric Clapton with Dire Straits

'We got banned by the South African Government back in 1979 I'm pleased to say. The best birthday party I've ever been to. Thank you very much.' MARK KNOPFLER, DIRE STRAITS

'Amazing Grace
How sweet the sound
That saved a wretch like me
I once was lost
But now I'm found
Was blind but now I see.'
– Amazing Grace JESSYE NORMAN

*America's great opera
singer Jessye Norman*

ISOLATE APARTHEID!

FAT BOYS

Keep smiling nelson!

FREE NELSON MANDELA

FREE MANDELA U.K.

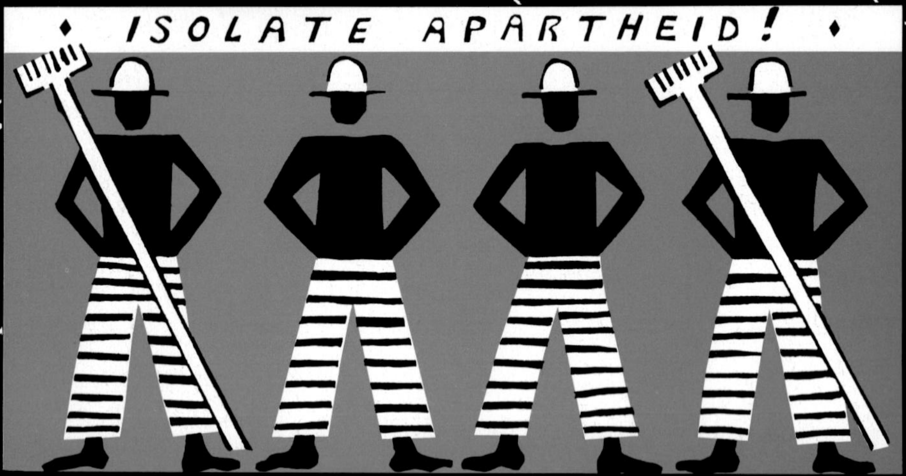

Jerry Dammers

STAY COOL BENI BOY FOR HIS

THE STRUGGLE IS MY LIFE!

June 11 1988.

WillyM → LONDONBEAT

LondonBeat

XXX

FYC

Best wishes
Mark Brzezicki

Stina o.

In Deep EFFECT

PRINCE MARKIE DEE

TONY LIAD ONE WORLD !

YOUSSOU

Happy Bday Nelson

Hugh Masekela

Amandla !

Free Nelson now

PORTRAITS

BY DAVIES AND STARR

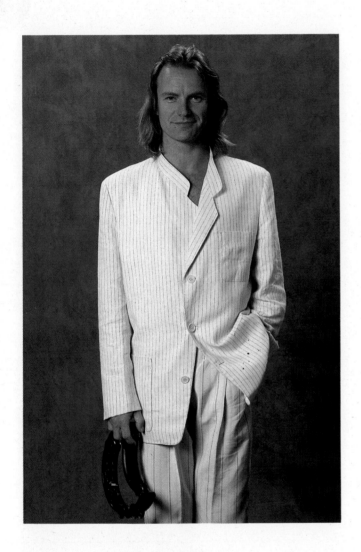

MIDGE URE
JOAN ARMATRADING
COURTNEY PINE
MEATLOAF

BILLY CONNOLLY
FISH
CHUBBY CHECKER AND HARRY BELAFONTE'S DAUGHTER
ACTRESS EMILY LLOYD

ASHFORD AND SIMPSON
WHOOPI GOLDBERG AND CORBIN BERNSEN
SLY DUNBAR AND ROBBIE SHAKESPEARE
DARYL HANNAH AND JACKSON BROWNE

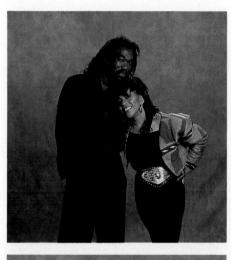

HARRY BELAFONTE
JOE COCKER
BRYAN ADAMS
GREGORY HINES

THE CONCERT

PRODUCERS
Elephant House Productions

FOR ELEPHANT HOUSE
Tony Hollingsworth – Live producer   Neville Bolt – Television executive producer   Ken O'Neill – Television executive director   Tisha Fein, Charles Brand – Producers   Sarah Lawrence, Alex Laird – Associate producers   Bibi Green – Assistant to producers   'John Gau – Programme consultant

PROMOTERS
Elephant House Productions & Marshall Arts for Freedom Productions Ltd

FOR MARSHALL ARTS
Barrie Marshall, Jenny Marshall, Doris Dixon

SHOW DESIGN
Mark Fisher and Jonathan Park of Fisher Park Ltd

LIGHTING DESIGN
Allen Branton, Kieran Healy, Chas Harrington

SOUND
Concert Sound Ltd

LIGHTING
Supermick Lights, Avo Lights, Seefactor, A.C. Lighting

RIGGING
Unusual Rigging Co

PRODUCION MANAGER
Roger Searle

STAGE MANAGER
Rik O'Brien

BACK STAGE MANAGER
Craig Stanley

STAGE CREW
Les Clifford & Stage Miracles

STAGE CONSTRUCTION
Mikkel Brogaard Design

GRAPHIC DESIGN
4i Collaboration

STAGE AND POSTER ART GIVEN BY ARTISTS
Sue Coe, Keith Haring, Malangatana Ngwenya, Mandy O'Shaughnessy, Cheryll Park, Ralph Steadman and the late John Muafangejo

VIDEO ARTS
Institute of Contemporary Arts

PYROTECHNICS
Le Maitre Fireworks

PRODUCTION TEAM
Sheilagh Searle, Tina Beanz, Howard Barrett, George England, Laureen Nolan, Carol Wafta Bolton, Fiona Macdonald, Mike Stewart, Ray Edwards, Cherry de Cordova, Dave Wilson, Michele Dix

THE BOOK

Portrait photography by Davies and Starr
Assisted by Eric Gauster and Tim Kent
Artists Co-ordination by Sophie and Laurel Lyon
Transportation and Studio construction by Alan 'Mega Assistant' Sheldon and Dave 'Mega Assistant' Hindley
Make-up by Maggie Baker

Panoramic photography by Laurie Lewis

Live photography by . . .
Adrian Boot, Eugene Adabari, Mike Putland, Paul Rider, Stefan Wallgren, Dave Wainwright, Laurie Lewis, Dario Mitidieri, Duncan Raban, Kevin Cummins, Alan Davidson, Tim Jarvis, Dave Hogan, Justin Thomas.

We would like to thank the following people and Company's for their invaluable help and assistance well beyond the realms of human endurance and normality . . .

Danielle, David, Roisine, Jason, Jim, Erika and Nicki at Retna, Daniel, Ginger and Tamara at Onyx, All at Lancaster Laboratories, All at Leeds Camera Centre, Gareth and Kerry at Keith Johnson Photographic, Pat at Polaroid, Kodak, Fuji, Afga and Polaroid for their generous donations of film, Michael, Don and Raymond from Roots, Brian Appel and Thom Oatman in N.Y.C., Stephanie for the T. Shirts, Ian at West One.

The designers would like to thank the following people for their help and enthusiasm in designing this book;

Roger Pring, Dorothy Tucker, Paul Levi, Gurdip Bhandal, Hannah Moore, Kevin Smith, Penny Phillips, Craig Cornock, David Mallott, Rob Partridge, Brian Rooney, Colin Woodman.

Roy, Neville and Kathy at Jigsaw Graphics, John Price Studios, Abacus Printing Co. Ltd, Colyer Graphics, Lizzie at Amwell Street.

PICTURE CREDITS
t: top, b: bottom, c: centre, l: left, r: right

Mary Benson 11t, 12b, 17,; Adrian Boot 28t, 29t, 44-5, 47, 48. 49, 55, 58b, 59, 60, 61, 67, 68, 69, 70, 71, 73b, 74, 78r, 79b, 82, 84-5, 87, 88, 89b, 90, 91, 92, 93, 86t, 97, 98, 99b, 101bl, 102, 105, 108t, 109, 114b, 122, 123, 129, 135tl; Kevin Cummins 36tr, 36b, 38, 39, 40t, 40c, 41; Alan Davidson 36tl, 37bl, 40b; Chalkie Davies 58t, 141-159; P.K.A. Gaeshwe (Umtata) 12t; IDAF (International Defence Aid Fund) 8, 9, 10, 11t, 11b, 12b, 12, 14, 15, 16, 17, 18, 19, 20, 21, 22, 23, 25, 25; Tim Jarvis 72-3, 100, 112, 113b, 114t, 133; Laurie Lewis 6-7, 28-9, 29b, 31, 32, 33, 34-5, 42, 43, 52-3, 56, 62-3, 83, 106-7, 110-1, 120-1; Dario Mitidieri 57, 64, 80-1, 99t, 101br, 103, 113t, 117, 118t, 119, 132t, 134, 136-7; Malangatana Ngwenya 30; Mandy O'Shaughnessy of Kwatz 138-9; Michael Putland 37br, 51, 130-1, 135tr, 135b; Duncan Raban 65b, 78t, 78c, 79tl, 95, 101t, 114c, 132b; Paul Rider 50, 54, 75, 77, 78bl, 89t, 96b, 118b, 124, 125, 126-7, 127br; Paul Roberts 115; David Waianright 37tl, 3tr, 81t, 81br; Roy Williams 65t, 108b, 127t. Every effort has been made to credit all photographs accurately. We apologise for any errors or omissions.

The Directors of Freedom Productions Limited and the Executive Committee of the Anti-Apartheid Movement would like to thank all those who helped ensure the success of the Nelson Mandela 70th Birthday Tribute and in particular:
Elephant House Productions
Marshall Arts
Jerry Dammers and all Artists Against Apartheid
The staff and volunteers of the AAM
We would also like to express our appreciation to Michael Rainbird Publishing Ltd and Penguin Books for the tremendous effort required to secure the publication of 'Free Nelson Mandela' for Nelson Mandela's 70th Birthday.

For further information write to the 'Nelson Mandela: Freedom at 70' Campaign, 13 Mandela Street, London NW1 0DW, England.